ZAIKA

Kashmiri Pandit Cuisine

ZAIKA

Kashmiri Pandit Cuisine

Sonya Atal Sapru

HarperCollins *Publishers* India

HarperCollins *Publishers* India Pvt Ltd
7/16 Ansari Road, Daryaganj, New Delhi 110 002

Copyright © Sonya Atal Sapru 1999
First published 1999 by
HarperCollins *Publishers* India

Sonya Atal Sapru asserts the moral right
to be identified as the author of this work

All rights reserved. No part of this publication may be reproduced, stored in a retrieval system, or transmitted, in any form, or by any means, electronic or mechanical, photocopying, recording or otherwise, without the prior permission of the publishers.

ISBN 81-7223-341-8

Printed in India by
Gopsons Papers Ltd
A-14 Sector 60
Noida 201 301

To my Papu

Ashok Atal

8.3.1939 - 18.5.1987

Contents

Acknowledgement	*viii*
Preface	*ix*
Introduction	*x*
How to plan a Kashmiri meal	1
Kashmiri garam masala	2
Non-vegetarian	5
Vegetarian	27
Dals & Rice	43
Chutneys, Raitas, Desserts	57

Acknowledgement

*I would like to thank my
mother-in-law, Gita Sapru
without whose help this book
would never have taken shape.*

Preface

Kashmiri Pandit cuisine has always had its devotees, but it owes its survival exclusively to the time honoured Indian practice of verbally handing down recipes through the generations.

As each mother retold the culinary secrets of her community to her daughter, Kashmiri Pandit cuisine subtly changed and evolved differently from household to household.

The essence of the rich, hearty, and yet subtly flavoured food has, however, remained untouched over time. This, then is *Zaika*, a compilation of original recipes gleaned from Kashmiri Pandit families, appropriately titled with the Urdu word for taste and flavour.

Introduction

The Kashmiri Pandits have been on the move for centuries. First forced out of their homeland by ethnic conflicts with the Mughals, their most recent exodus was in 1992-93.

Migrating from the extreme cold of the north to the relatively warmer climes of mid-north and central India; from a strongly meat influenced diet to one that accepts vegetables, legumes and pulses; from using spices that belonged exclusively to Kashmir, to incorporating ingredients from their new habitat; all these have had their inevitable effect on the cuisine.

Today's Kashmiri Pandit cuisine, therefore, is somewhat nouvelle in nature; modified to the conditions the Kashmiri Pandits find themselves in, but without forsaking the basic traditions that make the cuisine so celebrated.

The most important of these being the liberal use of aromatic spices, and the avoidance of onion and garlic.

The result is sheer flavour and richness.

A word of caution, though, these are not fast-to-cook convenience meals. Kashmiri cuisine demands long hours of marinating and cooking over a slow fire. So though *Zaika* has been devised with regard for modern conditions, I recommend that you use it only when you can single-mindedly devote yourself to the pursuit of culinary perfection.

My paternal great grandfather Pandit Pyarelal Atal with his wife Raj, and my grandfather Hira Lal [left] and grand aunt Kamla as children.

How to plan a Kashmiri Meal

A perfectly devised menu is one of the secrets of a great Kashmiri gastronomic experience. Here are some of the menus, combining complementary meat, lentil and vegetable recipes from this book with the appropriate sweet dish.

1. Methi machli dam
    Rogan josh
    Arhar dal
    Kar chaman
    Patta gobi ki sabzi
    Plain boiled rice
    Phirni

2. Khatti machi
    Passande
    Kabargah
    Chane ki dal
    Bhindi aloo dam
    Methi chaman
    Sarvari
    Meethi khubani

3. Gular kabab
    Yakhni
    Kaleji dam
    Khatti bhindi
    Urad ki dal
    Plain boiled rice
    Meethi guchi

4. Mattar keema
    Methi aloo
    Gobi ki sabzi
    Khamiri puri
    Passande
    Meethi dahi

Kashmiri garam masala
[Mixed aromatic spices]

Ingredients:

10 gms   cloves
10 gms   cinnamon
10 gms   black pepper
10 gms   black cumin
10 gms   bay leaves
100 gms   large cardamoms
2   pieces of mace
100 gms   cumin seeds

Method:

Roast all the ingredients together. Grind to a fine powder and bottle. [The masala can be stored in an airtight bottle for 3 to 4 months.]

My paternal great grandmother, Raj Atal, at her wedding at the turn of the last century.

Non-Vegetarian

Rogan josh
Koftas
Tamatar goli
Hare badam ka kalia
Khatti kaleji
Yakhni
Kabargah
Shaljum salan
Keema mattar
Stuffed passande dum
Gular kababs
Dhania ka shufta
Dum Kaleji
Methi machi dum
Khatti machi dum

Rogan josh

[A succulent mutton dish with a rich curd based gravy]

Serves: 6
Preparation time: 15 minutes
Cooking time: 1 hour 20 minutes

Ingredients:

1 kg	mutton [cut in small pieces with bones]
8–10 tbsp	clarified butter [ghee] or cooking oil
6 tbsp	curd [lightly beaten]
2 tsp	dry ginger powder
¼ tsp	asafoetida
3	bay leaves
2 tsp	red chilli powder
20	almonds [peeled and ground finely]
1 tbsp	poppy seeds [washed and ground finely]
3 tsp	aromatic spice [powdered]
8	small cardamoms [ground to a fine powder]
8	cloves [ground to a powder]
	salt to taste

For garnish:

10	almonds [soaked in water, skin removed and cut in slivers]

Method:

Heat the oil in a deep based pan. Pour in the curd, dry ginger powder, asafoetida and mutton pieces [on a high flame]. Stir the mutton pieces till it starts sticking to the pan and the curd is golden brown. Add 4 tablespoons of water in the pan and toss the meat around scraping the base of the pan till the meat browns evenly. [Keep adding the same quantity of water and stir frying at least 4 times].

Once the meat is browned evenly, add the bay leaves and red chilli powder and stir for a minute. Add 5 cups of water to the meat and let it come to a boil. Cover the pan and let it cook for 35 minutes on a slow flame. The meat should almost be cooked, and you should have a thick gravy. Add the ground almonds, poppy seeds, aromatic spices, cardamom, clove powder and salt. Cover the pan and let it simmer for 10 minutes by which time the dish should be cooked. Garnish with almond slivers.

Koftas

[Sausage shaped meat balls of fine mince cooked in curd]

Serves: 8
Preparation time: 15 minutes
Cooking time: 1 hour 15 minutes

Ingredients: [for koftas]

1 kg	mince [ground finely]
6 tbsp	thick curd
125 gms	mustard oil [smoked and cooled before cooking]
1" piece	fresh ginger [ground finely]
2 tbsp	poppy seeds [washed strained and ground finely]
2 tsp	dried coriander seed powder
1 tsp	asafoetida
1 tsp	cumin seed powder
1 tsp	red chilli powder
2 tsp	dry ginger powder
	salt to taste

For the gravy:

8-10 tbsp	clarified butter [ghee] or cooking oil
12 tbsp	curd
1 tsp	asafoetida
2 tsp	dry ginger powder
2 tsp	red chilli powder

Method:

Mix all the kofta spices with the minced meat and set the mixture aside for 30 minutes. Shape the mixture like sausages and keep them aside. To make the gravy, first heat the ghee or the oil in a large pan. Add the curd, asafoetida and dry ginger powder. Cook the mixture till the curd turns brown and the oil separates. [This should take about 30 minutes].

Add half the red chilli powder, stir for a minute and remove the pan from the fire. Now gently lower the koftas into the pan, keeping them separate from each other. Place the pan on a very low flame and cook for 10 minutes. Add approximately 2 tablespoons of water at a time and turning the koftas so that they don't crumble [Repeat this at least 4 to 5 times].

Add the remaining red chilli powder and let it cook for a minute, and pour 2 tablespoons of water. Continue cooking till the water has almost evaporated and the koftas are left with a slight gravy.

Tamatar Goli

[*Meatballs cooked in a tomato and curd gravy*]

Serves: 2
Preparation time: 30 minutes
Cooking time: 45 minutes

Ingredients: [for golis]

250 gms	fine minced meat
½ tsp	asafoetida
1¼ tsp	mustard oil [uncooked]
1½ tsp	thick curd
1 ½ tsp	dry ginger powder
½ tsp	red chilli powder
2 tsp	mixed aromatic spice
1 ½	piece of fresh ginger [cut in juliennes]
	salt to taste

For the gravy:

4 tsp	cooking oil
½ tsp	asafoetida
3 tsp	curd [lightly beaten]
1 ½ tsp	dry ginger powder
½ tsp	red chilli powder
4 tbsp	thick tomato puree

For garnish:

2 tsp	fresh ginger juliennes
2 tbsp	fresh coriander [chopped finely]

Method:

Mix the mince with the goli ingredients, and set aside for 30 minutes. Shape the mixture in small balls [approximately 2 cm in diameter] and keep aside. To make the gravy, heat the oil in a pan, and add asafoetida, curd and dry ginger powder. Cook this mixture till the curd turns golden brown and starts sticking to the base of the pan. Add 2 tablespoons of water and scrape the bottom of the pan [Repeat this 5 times] till the oil separates from the mixture.

Take the pan of the fire and gently place the golis side by side. Cook over a slow flame and keep turning the pan around without using a spatula, so as not to break the golis. Add the red chilli powder and gradually start browning the golis, by stirring very gently, once it starts sticking to the base of the pan add 2 tablespoons of water along with the tomato puree [Keep adding the same quantity of water till the golis have browned completely]. This should take 10 minutes. The golis should be cooked, and left with a thickish gravy. Garnish with ginger juliennes and fresh coriander.

My husband's paternal grandmother, Kishanpati Sapru, whose meticulous record of household recipes discovered whilst rummaging through an old cabin trunk, were the inspiration for this book.

Hare Badam ka Kalia
[Mutton cooked in milk with green almonds]

Serves: 4
Preparation time: 10 minutes
Cooking time: 1 hour

Ingredients

1 kg	mutton [cut in small pieces with their bones]
10 tbsp	cooking oil
¼ tsp	asafoetida
2 tsp	dry ginger powder
4 cups	boiled milk
25	green almonds [fried and crispy]
5 tbsp	fresh cream [whipped]
12 tbsp	curd
5	cloves [powdered]
	salt to taste [add it after the dish has been cooked because the milk will curdle if you put the salt in first]

If you want the gravy to be yellow in colour, omit the milk and the cream and add water instead with 1½ tsp turmeric powder.

2 tsp	mixed aromatic spices
8	green cardamoms [seeds powdered, and outer skin discarded]
	a pinch of saffron

Method:

Heat the oil in a deep based pan. Add asafoetida, dry ginger powder and the mutton pieces. When the meat starts browning, add half the milk and let it simmer on a low flame with lid on the pan for 10 – 15 minutes. The meat should be almost tender by now.

Gradually add the green almonds with the remaining milk, curd and whipped cream, and stir. Leave it on a slow flame till the gravy gets thick. Now add the cloves, salt, mixed aromatic spices, cardamoms and saffron, and keep stirring gently. Leave it on a slow fire to cook further till the meat is absolutely tender.

KHATTI KALEJI
[Sour meat liver]

Serves: 4
Preparation time: 10 minutes
Cooking time: 40 minutes

Ingredients :

500 gms	mutton liver
6 tsp	cooking oil
1 tsp	asafoetida
1 tsp	dry ginger powder
6 tbsp	curd
1 tsp	turmeric powder
¾ tsp	red chilli powder
2	lemons [juice extracted]
3	green chillies [chopped finely]
1½ tsp	juliennes of ginger
2 tsp	mixed aromatic spice
½ tsp	fennel seeds*
½ tsp	fenugreek*
½ tsp	cloves*
	salt to taste

*roasted and powdered

For garnish:

Finely chopped fresh green coriander.

Method:

Heat the oil in a deep pan. Add asafoetida, dry ginger powder and curd. Stir for 10 minutes till the curd is slightly brown in colour. Then add the liver, turmeric powder, chilli powder and salt, and stir for a few minutes. Add 2 cups of water, cover the pan and let it cook over a small flame till the liver gets tender. [This should take approximately 10 minutes]. Add the lime juice extract, chopped green chillies, ginger juliennes, mixed aromatic spice and the roasted and powdered fennel seed, fenugreek and lovange, with approximately 3/4 cup of water and let it cook for 5 minutes. Garnish with freshly cut coriander.

My husband, Rakesh [centre] and his younger brother Nirukt [left] at their much delayed thread ceremony, [janeu] confirming their Brahmanical rites with a Kashmiri Pandit [priest]. The thread ceremony is essential for all Brahmins and is usually performed at a much younger age.

Yakhni
[*Mutton pieces cooked in milk*]

Serves: 4
Preparation time: 10 minutes
Cooking time: 1 hour

Ingredients:

1 kg	mutton [cut in small pieces with bones]
6 tbsp	cooking oil
8 cups	boiled milk [cooled]
2"	cinnamon stick
1 ½ tsp	dry ginger powder
10	small green cardamoms
3 tsp	fennel seeds [powdered]
4	bay leaves
8	dried red chillies
	a pinch of saffron
	salt to taste [add it after the dish has been cooked as the milk will curdle if you put the salt first]

Method:

Heat the oil in a deep based pan. As it starts smoking, add the milk, meat, cinnamon stick, dry ginger powder, cardamoms, fennel powder and bay leaves and cook on a medium flame till the meat is tender and the milk has dried to form a thinnish gravy.

[You must remember to keep stirring as the milk is liable to stick to the base of the pan]. This should take 35 to 40 minutes. Now add the salt, whole red chillies and the saffron and cook for 10 minutes and your yakhni should be ready.

Kabargah
[Mutton chops cooked in milk & deep fried in chick pea flour batter]

Serves: 4
Preparation time: 10 minutes
Cooking time: 40 minutes

Ingredients:

1 kg	mutton chops
¾ kg	milk
250 gms	chick pea flour [sifted, and prepare batter which is not too thick]
2 tsp	red chilli powder
2 tsp	turmeric powder
2 tsp	mixed aromatic spice
2 tsp	fennel seeds powder
½ tsp	asafoetida cooking oil for deep frying
8	cloves
8	large cardamoms
1½"	cinnamon stick
5	bay leaves
5 tsp	fennel seeds
	[tie the last 5 ingredients together in a muslin cloth]

Method:

Put the milk, mutton chops and the spices that have been tied in a muslin cloth to boil in a pressure cooker on a medium flame. [It should take approximately 15 minutes for the milk to dry and the chops to get tender]. Mix the chickpea batter with the red chilli powder, turmeric powder, mixed aromatic spices, fennel powder and asafoetida. Dip the chops in the batter, and deep fry to a golden brown.

Shaljum salan
[*Mutton cooked with turnips*]

Serves: 4
Preparation time: 15 minutes
Cooking time: 50 minutes

Ingredients:

½ kg	mutton [cut in pieces with bones]
4 tbsp	cooking oil
3 tbsp	curd [lightly beaten]
¼ tsp	asafoetida
2 tsp	dry ginger powder
250 gms	turnips [cut in quarters and deep fried till golden brown]
1 tsp	sugar
1 ½ tsp	mixed aromatic spice
2 tsp	red chilli powder to taste
	salt to taste
8	cardamoms [skinned and powdered]
5 tsp	fennel seeds
2	large black cardamoms
2"	piece cinnamon stick
8	cloves
	[The last 4 ingredients are to be tied in a muslin cloth]

For garnish:

2 tbsp fresh green coriander [chopped finely]

Method:

Heat the oil in a deep based pan. Add the curd, asafoetida and dry ginger powder and let it brown. Add the mutton and cook on a medium flame.

As the meat starts sticking to the base of the pan add 2 to 3 tbsps of water at a time and scrape the base of the pan, wait for a couple of minutes and repeat at least 5 times, till the colour of the meat has turned deep brown [It takes approximately 35 minutes].

Now take the spices that are tied in the muslin cloth and immerse into the pan with meat with 6 cups of water, and leave on a slow flame till the meat is half cooked.

Add the turnips, sugar, mixed aromatic spice, red chilli powder, salt and 3 to 4 cups of water. Cook for another 15 minutes, till the meat and the turnips are tender. Remove the muslin cloth with mixed spices, [squeezing it fully] sprinkle the powdered cardamom and let it simmer on a low flame for 5 minutes. Garnish with freshly chopped coriander.

KEEMA MATTAR
[Minced meat cooked with peas]

Serves: 3
Preparation time: 10 minutes
Cooking time: 50 minutes

Ingredients:

300 gms	mince meat
300 gms	peas [boiled]
5 tbsp	cooking oil
1 ½ tsp	asafoetida
1 ¼ tsp	dry ginger powder
4 tbsp	curd [lightly beaten]
2 tsp	juliennes of ginger
1 tsp	turmeric powder
2 tsp	mixed aromatic spice
½ tsp	red chilli powder
2 tsp	coriander powder
	salt to taste

Method:

Heat the oil in a deep based pan. Add asafoetida, dry ginger powder and curd along with the mince. Once the mince browns and sticks to the base of the pan, keep adding 4 tablespoons of water and scraping the base of the pan [Repeat this at least 4 to 5 times]. Once the mince has browned [approximately 35 minutes] add the boiled peas, ginger juliennes, turmeric powder, mixed aromatic spice, red chilli powder, coriander powder, salt and 2 cups of water, cook for approximately 10 minutes, by which time your keema mattar should be cooked and ready to serve.

Stuffed passande dum

[Passande are boneless pieces of meat from the shoulder of the goat which has been cut and flattened to the size of the palm]

Serves: 4
Preparation time: 30 minutes
Cooking time: 1 hour

Ingredients:

½ kg	passande
10 - 12	dried plums [soaked overnight, retain the puree and discard the seeds]
30	almonds [soaked overnight, the skin removed and cut into juliennes]
8 tsp	raisins
4 tsp	mixed aromatic spice
	salt to taste
12 tbsp	curd
3 tsp	dry ginger powder
½ tsp	asafoetida
½	nutmeg [powdered]
10	green cardamoms
6 tsp	juliennes of ginger
1 ½ tsp	red chilli powder
6 tbsp	cooking oil
	cooking twine [to tie the passande]

Method: [for the stuffing]

Take the plum puree, almond juliennes, raisins, ½ tsp of the mixed aromatic spice, half of the red chilli powder and a little salt, and mix together in bowl. Now take one passanda at a time and add the above mixture to it carefully, roll it like a sausage and tie the cooking twine around.

Method: [for cooking]

Take cooking oil in a deep pan, and put over a high flame, as it starts smoking, add the curd, dry ginger powder and the asafoetida, and cook for 10 minutes till the mixture starts browning. Gently add the passande side by side in the pan and for a minute or two. Slowly sprinkle the powdered nutmeg, cardamoms, ginger juliennes, the balance aromatic spice, red chilli powder and salt.

Cover the pan for about 40 minutes, stirring gently from time to time so as not to break the passandas. By now the passandas should be cooked and very tender. Cut the twine and place in the dish side by side. Garnish with the balance of the stuffing ingredients.

Gaura Sapru,
A portrait of an ancestor from my husband's family, found in an old chest of photographs, which was salvaged from the ancestral home in Allahabad.

Gular kababs
[Fine minced meat with a stuffing]

Serves: 3
Preparation time: 15 minutes
Cooking time: 25 minutes

Ingredients: [for the kabab]

250 gms	mince meat
65 gms	split gram lentil [yellow channa dal]
3 tsp	curd
1 tsp	clarified butter [ghee]
1	dried fig
1 tbsp	poppy seeds
1	small mace
1	small nutmeg
1 tsp	fresh ginger
1 tsp	cumin seeds
2	fresh green chillies
1 tbsp	corn flour
	a pinch of salt
	a pinch of saffron
	a pinch of red chilli powder

[for the filling]

2	oranges [remove the segments and peel the skin]
3	green chillies [cut finely]
20	raisins [soaked in warm water for 5 minutes and dried]
1 tbsp	fresh ginger [cut in small pieces]
	cooking oil for frying

Method:

Mix all the ingredients [upto the cornflour] together for the kabab in a deep pan with 6 cups of water and cook on a high flame, stirring continuously. As the mixture is tender and the water has dried, take off the fire, and grind to a fine paste and add the cornflour, salt, saffron and red chilli powder. Mix the ingredients for the filling of the kabab and keep aside. Flatten small portions of the mince meat in the palm of your hand and place a teaspoon of the mixture in the centre and form into round balls. Deep fry to a golden brown and serve hot.

DHANIA KA SHUFTA
[Minced meat cooked with fresh green coriander]

Serves: 4
Prepartion time: 25 minutes
Cooking time: 45 minutes

Ingredients:

½ kg	mince meat
4 tbsps	clarified oil or cooking oil
1 ½ cup	peas [shelled]
2 tsp	dry ginger powder
¼ tsp	asafoetida
12 tbsps	curd [lightly beaten]
1 ½ tsp	turmeric powder
2 tsp	red chilli powder
	salt to taste
½ kg	fresh green coriander [chopped finely]
2 tbsp	ginger juliennes
2 tbsp	raisins
10	almonds [cut in juliennes]
6	green chillies [cut finely]
2	oranges [peeled- the segments remaining as whole]

Method:

Heat the cooking oil in a deep based pan. Add the dry ginger powder, asafoetida, curd and mince and keep stirring till the mince turns brown, by adding 4 tablespoons of water. Keep stirring. Once it is nicely browned, add the turmeric powder and red chilli powder, salt and peas. Stir for a minute or two. Add 5 cups of water to the mince, cover the pan with a lid and cook on a medium flame.

Once the mince is cooked, add the fresh green coriander, juliennes of ginger, raisins and almonds and green chillies [Cook till the smell of fresh green coriander does not remain]. Lastly, add the peeled oranges and cook for another two minutes, and serve.

Dum Kaleji
[*Mutton liver cooked in curd*]

Serves: 2
Preparation time: 5 minutes
Cooking time: 40 minutes

Ingredients:

250 gms	mutton liver diced in 1" cubes
4 tbsp	cooking oil
4 tbsp	curd [lightly beaten]
¼ tsp	asafoetida
1 tsp	dry ginger powder
2 tsp	ginger juliennes
2 ½ tsp	mixed aromatic spice

Method:

Heat the oil in a deep based pan. Add the curd, asafoetida and dry ginger powder, and let it cook on a medium flame. Gradually add the diced liver to the pan and brown. As it starts sticking to the base of the pan add 4 tablespoons of water and keep browning [Repeat 3 times]. Add the ginger juliennes with approximately 5 teaspoons of water, and let it stand for 10 minutes, till the water dries. Finally, add the mixed aromatic spice and cook for a minute or two and remove from fire.

METHI MACHI DUM

[Fish cooked in fenugeek]

Serves: 4 - 5
Preparation time: 10 minutes
Cooking time: 20 minutes

Ingredients:

400 gms	fish [cut in large cubes]
4 tsp	cooking oil
4 tbsp	mustard oil [for frying the fish]
¼ tsp	asafoetida
½ tsp	cumin seeds [whole]
6 tsp	spinach [boiled, ground to a thick paste]
½ tsp	turmeric powder
½ tsp	chilli powder
2 tsp	fenugreek powder or
2 tsp	fresh fenugreek [boiled, ground to a thick paste]
1 ½ tsp	ginger juliennes
2 tsp	mixed aromatic spice
	salt to taste

Method:

Deep fry the fish in the mustard oil, and keep aside. Heat the cooking oil in a pan, and add the asafoetida and cumin seeds, stir for a minute. Add the boiled spinach and stir for 5 minutes. Now add the turmeric powder, red chilli powder, salt and fenugreek and stir for a couple of minutes. Add about 6 tablespoons of water, the fried fish along with the ginger juliennes and let it cook on slow flame for 5 minutes. Sprinkle the mixed aromatic spice on the fish curry and serve hot.

KHATTI MACHI DUM
[*Sour fish curry cooked in curd*]

Serves: 3
Preparation time: 10 minutes
Cooking time: 25 minutes

Ingredients:

250 gms	fish [cut in large cubes]
4 tsp	cooking oil
4 tbsp	mustard oil [for frying the fish]
¼ tsp	asafoetida
¼ tsp	cumin seeds
4 tsp	curd [lightly beaten]
¾ tsp	turmeric powder
½ tsp	red chilli powder
1½ tsp	mixed aromatic spice
2	green chillies [finely chopped]
1 tsp	ginger juliennes
2 tsp	fresh coriander [finely chopped]
½ tsp	fenugreek [roasted]
½ tsp	fennel seeds [roasted]
½ tsp	cloves [roasted]
	[the last three ingredients ground to a fine powder]
1	lemon [juice extracted]
	salt to taste

Method:

Deep fry the fish in mustard oil and keep aside. In another pan heat the cooking oil and add the asafoetida and cumin seeds and cook for a minute. Now add the whipped curd with turmeric powder and chilli powder, and stir for 2 minutes.

Gradually add the fried pieces of fish, mixed aromatic spices, chopped green chillies, ginger juliennes, fresh green coriander with the fenugreek, fennel and lovange mixture. Add 6 tablespoons of water. Leave it to cook on a slow flame till the fish is tender. Finally add the lime juice extract and salt to the curry, and cook for a minute or two. The dish should have a thinnish gravy.

Jagdish Narain Sapru [my father-in-law] sitting on his mother's lap with his father on the left at his janeo [thread ceremony], (1938)

Vegetarian

Kathal kababs
Dum aloo
Methi chaman
Kar chaman
Khatti bhindi
Nadru ki kurkuri
Patta gobi ki sabzi
Bhindi aloo dum
Khatti arvi
Palak baigan ki sabzi
Khatta zameen kand
Khatte baigan

KATHAL KABABS
[Jack fruit kababs]

Serves: 2-3
Preparation time: 10 minutes
Cooking time: 20 minutes

Ingredients:

350 gms	jackfruit
¾ cup	chickpea dal
2"	cinnamon stick
8	cloves
2	bay leaves
5	large cardamoms
10 gms	ginger
2	green chillies [finely chopped]
1 tsp	mixed aromatic spice
¼ tsp	asafoetida
½ tsp	red chilli powder
3 tsp	fresh coriander [finely chopped]
8 tbsp	cooking oil [for deep frying the kababs]
	salt to taste

Method:

Put the jackfruit along with the chickpea dal, cinnamon, cloves, bay leaves, cardamoms, ginger, green chillies and salt in a pressure cooker with approximately 2 cups of water to boil. [It should take 10 minutes for the water to dry].

Grind the above mixture to a fine paste. Now add the mixed aromatic spice, asafoetida, red chilli powder and chopped green coriander to the above mixture, and mix well. Form into medium sized kababs and deep fry. Serve hot.

Dum aloo

[Potatoes cooked in curd]

Serves: 3
Preparation time: 15 minutes
Cooking time: 50 minutes

Ingredients:

250 gms	potatoes [round, equal size]
5 tsp	cooking oil
15 tbsps	cooking oil [for frying]
¼ tsp	asafoetida
1 ¼ tsp	dry ginger powder
4 tsp	curd [lightly beaten]
¾ tsp	red chilli powder
	salt to taste
1 ½ tsp	ginger juliennes
1 ¼ tsp	mixed aromatic spice
6	green cardamoms [powdered]

Method:

Boil the potatoes till almost tender, then peel and prick each potato with a toothpick all over. Deep fry the potatoes to a darkish brown, and keep aside. In another pan heat the oil and asafoetida, dry ginger powder and curd and cook for 10 to 15 minutes on a medium flame, till the curd starts sticking to the base of the pan. Keep stirring and scraping the stuck curds all the time by adding 3 teaspoons of water [Repeat this 4 times till the curd is deep brown]. Add the potatoes, red chilli powder, salt, ginger juliennes and cook on a slow flame for 10 minutes. Now add the mixed aromatic spices, powdered green cardamoms and cook for 5 minutes. The dish should have very little gravy.

Methi chaman
[Cottage cheese cooked in fenugeek]

Serves: 2
Preparation time: 10 minutes
Cooking time: 30 minutes

Ingredients:

200 gms	cottage cheese [cut in 1 ½" cubes]
3 tsp	spinach [boiled and ground to a paste]
3 cups	warm water
	salt to taste
¼ tsp	turmeric powder [for the warm water]
½ tsp	asafoetida
1 tsp	cumin seeds
3 tsp	dry fenugreek [powdered] or
1 tsp	fresh fenugreek [boiled and ground to a thick paste]
¼ tsp	red chilli powder
2 tsp	ginger juliennes
1 ¼ tsp	mixed aromatic spices
½ tsp	fennel seed [powdered]
6	green cardamoms [powdered]
2 tbsp	cooking oil
10 tbsp	cooking oil [for frying]

Method:

Fry the cottage cheese till the edges are golden brown. In another pan take 3 cups of warm water, add a pinch of salt and turmeric powder and bring this to a boil and keep aside. Now immerse the fried pieces of cottage cheese and leave for 5 minutes [this helps in softening the cottage cheese]. Heat the cooking oil in a pan, and add the asafoetida, cumin seeds and let it splatter. Add the boiled spinach and cook till the oil separates, then add the fenugreek and cook for a few minutes. Now add the turmeric powder, red chilli powder, salt and 10 tablespoons of water. Drain the water from the cottage cheese, and gently add to the pan containing the spinach and fenugreek mixture, add the ginger juliennes and leave it to simmer on a low flame. Now finally add the mixed aromatic spice, fennel seed powder and the cardamom powder and leave to cook for 5 minutes on a slow flame, by which time your chaman should be ready.

KAR CHAMAN

[Cottage cheese and peas cooked in a tomato gravy]

Serves: 2
Preparation time: 10 minutes
Cooking time: 25 minutes

Ingredients:

200 gms	cottage cheese [cut in ½"cubes]
5 tbsp	cooking oil
10 tbsp	cooking oil [for frying]
3 cups	warm water
	salt to taste
3/4 tsp	turmeric powder [for the warm water]
¼ tsp	asafoetida
¼ tsp	cumin seeds
3 tbsp	tomato puree
½ cup	peas [shelled and boiled]
¼ tsp	turmeric powder
¼ tsp	red chilli powder
2 tsp	ginger juliennes
12	green chillies [finely chopped]
2 tsp	mixed aromatic spices
½ tsp	sugar

For garnish:

4 tsp   fresh green coriander [finely cut]

Method:

Fry the pieces of the cottage cheese till the edges are golden brown. In a pan take 3 cups of warm water, add a pinch of salt, half the turmeric powder and bring this to a boil and keep aside. Immerse the fried cottage cheese pieces, and leave this for 5 minutes [This helps in softening the cottage cheese]. Heat the cooking oil in a pan, and add the asafoetida, cumin seeds and let it splatter. Now add the tomato puree and let it cook for 5 minutes, stirring all the time. Drain the water from the cottage cheese and add to the pan with puree. Also add the boiled peas, stir for a minute or two so that the cottage cheese does not break. Add the remaining turmeric powder, red chilli powder, ginger juliennes, green chillies, mixed aromatic spice, sugar with approximately half cup of water and salt, and stir for 10 minutes. There should be a slight gravy in the dish. Garnish with fresh green coriander.

KHATTI BHINDI
[Sour okra cooked in curd]

Serves: 2
Preparation time: 10 minutes
Cooking time: 20 minutes

Ingredients:

250 gms	okra
3 tbsp	cooking oil
6 tbsp	cooking oil [for frying]
¼ tsp	asafoetida
¼ tsp	cumin seeds
4 tbsp	curd [lightly beaten]
½ tsp	turmeric power
½ tsp	red chilli powder
1 ½ tsp	mixed aromatic spice
¼ tsp	fennel seeds*
¼ tsp	cloves*
¼ tsp	fenugreek*
2 tsp	fresh ginger juliennes
1 tsp	green chillies [cut finely]
1 ½ tbsp	lime juice
1 ½ tsp	fresh mint [cut finely]
	salt to taste

*roasted and powdered

For garnish:

2 tsp   fresh mint [finely cut]

Method:

Snip both ends of the okra and make small slits on two opposite sides. Let it remain whole. Now deep fry the okra till golden brown. Take another pan and heat the cooking oil. Add the asafoetida and the cumin seeds and let it splatter. Add the whipped curd and stir till it turns brown. Now add the okra and the turmeric powder, red chilli powder, mixed aromatic spices, fennel seed powder lovange, fenugreek powdered spice, salt and stir for a minute or two. Add ¾ cup of water, chopped mint, juliennes of ginger and green chillies. Cover to cook for 10 minutes till you get a gravy. Finally, add the lime juice extract and cook for 2 minutes and remove from fire. Garnish with the chopped mint.

NADRU KI KURKURI
[Crispy lotus stem]

Serves: 3
Preparation time: 20 minutes
Cooking time: 15 minutes

Ingredients:

1	stick lotus stem, 12" to 14"
1 cup	cooking oil [for frying]
	salt to taste
	red chilli powder to taste

Method:

Scrape the lotus stem and chop diagonally, like thick potato wafers. Boil the wafers till tender, drain the water and spread to dry. Take the cooking oil in a pan and deep fry to golden brown. Sprinkle red chilli powder and salt to taste. Serve hot.

Late Maj. General H.L. Atal, my paternal grandfather. Educated at Sandhurst and commissioned into the 16th Cavalry in 1925, a connoisseur in his own right.

PATTA GOBI KI SABZI
[*Cabbage*]

Serves: 4
Preparation time: 10 minutes
Cooking time: 30 minutes

Ingredients:

1 kg	cabbage [cut in large pieces]
½ tsp	asafoetida
½ tsp	cumin seeds
1 tsp	sugar
1 tsp	red chilli powder
1 tsp	coriander powder
1 tsp	mixed aromatic spice
3 tbsps	cooking oil
	salt to taste

For garnish:

4 tbsps   fresh coriander [finely cut]

Method:

Heat oil in a pan, and add the asafoetida and cumin seeds. Once it splatters, add the cut cabbage. Cover the pan with a lid and let it cook for 5 minutes. Then add the sugar and all the spices and stir for 2 to 3 minutes, with 2 cups of water. Stir once again, put the lid on the pan and let the cabbage cook over a small flame, till it is tender. Garnish with freshly chopped coriander.

BHINDI ALOO DUM
[Okra and potato]

Serves: 3
Preparation time: 10 minutes
Cooking time: 35 minutes

Ingredients:

250 gms	okra [washed and both ends snipped]
400 gms	potato [peeled and sliced in halves]
3 tbsp	cooking oil [for cooking]
5 tbsp	cooking oil [for deep frying]
¼ tsp	asafoetida
1 tsp	dry ginger powder
3 tbsp	curd [lightly beaten]
½ tsp	red chilli powder
1 ½ tsp	mixed aromatic spices
8	small green cardamoms [powdered]
1 tbsp	juliennes of ginger
	salt to taste

Method:

Deep fry both the okra and potatoes [separately] till golden brown, and keep aside. Heat cooking oil in another pan and add the asafoetida, dry ginger powder and the whipped curd, and cook till the mixture turns golden brown. Gradually add the fried okra and the potatoes, along with red chilli powder, mixed aromatic spice, powdered cardamoms, juliennes of ginger, salt and approximately 2 cups of water. Cover the pan and cook on a slow flame for 10 minutes, by which time the vegetables will be tender and you are left with a slight gravy.

KHATTI ARVI
[Sour yam]

Serves: 4
Preparation time: 25 minutes
Cooking time: 20 minutes

Ingredients:

½ kg	yam [cut in pieces and boiled till almost tender]
3 tbsp	mustard oil
3 tbsp	cooking oil
¼ tsp	asafoetida
2 tsp	dry ginger powder
6 tbsp	curd [lightly beaten]
2 tsp	mixed aromatic spices
¼ tsp	red chilli powder
6	green chillies [chopped finely]
1 tsp	fresh ginger juliennes
3 tsp	fresh lemon juice extract
½ tsp	fennel seeds*
½ tsp	cloves*
½ tsp	fenugreek*
	salt to taste

*roasted and powdered

for garnish:

4 tsp   fresh mint [chopped finely]

Method:

Smoke the mustard oil in a deep based pan till very hot. Add the asafoetida, dry ginger powder and the lightly beaten curd and slowly brown to a very pale colour. In another pan heat the cooking oil and deep fry the yam to a golden brown. Now add the fried yam to the pan containing the curd mixture along with the other ingredients. Cook till you get a thickish gravy. Garnish with chopped mint.

Palak baigan ki sabzi
[Spinach and aubergines]

Serves: 4
Preparation time: 15 minutes
Cooking time: 20 minutes

Ingredients:

250 gms	*spinach [chopped coarsely]*
250 gms	*aurbergines [cut in pieces]*
3 tbsp	*cooking oil*
¼ tsp	*asafoetida*
½ tsp	*cumin seeds*
	salt to taste
¼ tsp	*turmeric powder*
¼ tsp	*red chilli powder*
1 tsp	*coriander powder*
½ tsp	*mixed aromatic spices*

Method:

Heat oil in a deep based pan, and add the asafoetida and cumin seeds. Once it starts splattering, add the cut spinach, and let it cook for 5 minutes till the water has almost dried. Now add the cut pieces of aubergines, salt, turmeric powder, red chilli powder, coriander powder, mixed aromatic spices, and cover the pan with a lid and let it cook for another 10 minutes on a slow flame. Once the aubergines are tender the dish is ready to be served.

KHATTA ZAMEEN KAND
[Sour elephant's foot]

Serves: 5
Preparation time: 35 minutes
Cooking time: 35 minutes

Ingredients:

½ kg	zameen kand [cut 1" flat & ¼" thick pieces, and boiled for 30 minutes or till tender]
100 gms	mustard oil
100 gm	cooking oil
¼ tsp	asafoetida
6 tbsp	curd [lightly beaten]
2 tsp	dry ginger powder
2 tsp	mixed aromatic spices
¼ tsp	red chilli powder
6	green chillies [finely chopped]
1 tsp	ginger juliennes
3 tsp	lemon juice extract
½ tsp	fennel seeds*
½ tsp	cloves*
½ tsp	fenugreek powder*
	salt to taste

*roasted and powdered

for garnish:

4 tsp fresh mint [chopped finely]

Method:

Smoke the mustard oil in a deep based pan till very hot. Add the asafoetida, beaten curd and dry ginger powder. Slowly brown to a very pale colour [The curd should retain its colour]. In another pan deep fry the elephant's foot to a golden brown. Add the fried elephant's foot to the curd mixture, along with the remaining ingredients and cook till you get a thickish gravy. Garnish with the freshly chopped mint.

KHATTE BAIGAN
[Sour aubergines]

Serves: 4
Preparation time: 10 minutes
Cooking time: 15 minutes

For garnish:
2 tbsp   fresh mint [finely chopped]

Ingredients:

500 gms	aubergines [cut in 1" pieces]
3 tbsp	cooking oil
½ tsp	asafoetida
½ tsp	cumin seeds
½ tsp	turmeric powder
½ tsp	red chilli powder
	salt to taste
4 tsp	lime juice extract
1 tsp	ginger juliennes
4	green chillies [finely chopped]
1 ½ tsp	fresh mint [finely chopped]
½ tsp	fennel seeds*
½ tsp	cloves*
½ tsp	fenugreek*
2 tsp	mixed aromatic spices

*roasted and powdered

Method:

Heat the cooking oil in a deep pan, and add the asafoetida and cumin seeds. Gradually add the aubergines, stirring occasionally so that it does not stick to the base of the pan, and let it cook for 10 minutes on a low flame. Now add the turmeric powder, red chilli powder, salt and about ¾ cup of water and cover the pan till the aubergines are almost tender. Cook on a low flame. Finally, add the lemon juice extract, ginger juliennes, green chillies, mint, aromatic spices, fennel, lovange, fenugreek powder. Give it a stir for a minute or two without breaking the aubergines. Remove from the fire and garnish with the remaining mint.

Dals & Rice

Urad dal
Channe ki dal
Shaljum dal
Khatti arhar dal
Arhar dal
Sarvari
Bhasbhatta
Khameeri puri
Baria

Urad dal
[Snow white lentil]

Serves: 4
Preparation time: 5 minutes
Cooking time: 20 minutes

Ingredients:

1 ¼ cup	snow white lentil
1 tsp	ginger juliennes
3	green chillies [finely chopped]
	salt to taste

for garnish:

1 ½ tbsp	clarified butter
¼ tsp	asafoetida
¼ tsp	cumin seeds
½ tsp	red chilli powder

Method:

Put the snow white lentil in approximately 5 cups of water [not in a pressure cooker] and leave to cook. When the lentil is slightly tender add the salt, ginger juliennes, and green chillies and leave to simmer till it is cooked [Each grain should be separate]. Take a small pan and heat the clarified butter, when it is hot add the asafoetida and cumin seeds. As it starts splattering, take off the fire and add the red chilli powder and stir for a second. Pour over the cooked lentil as garnish.

Channe ki dal
[Chick pea dal]

Serves: 4
Preparation time: 5 minutes
Cooking time: 20 minutes

Ingredients:

1 ½ cup	chickpea dal
1 tsp	sugar
½ tsp	turmeric powder
½ tsp	salt
2	green chillies [finely chopped]
3 tsp	mint [finely chopped]
1 tsp	ginger juliennes

for garnish:

1 ½ tsp	clarified butter
¼ tsp	asafoetida
¼ tsp	cumin seeds
½ tsp	red chilli powder

Method:

Put the chickpea dal, sugar, turmeric powder and approximately 8 to 10 cups of water in a pressure cooker for approximately 15 minutes. After the dal is cooked, half mash it with a whisk. Now add the green chillies, mint and ginger juliennes and dal with 12 tablespoons of water and let it cook for 5 minutes. Take a small pan and heat the clarified butter. When it is hot add the asafoetida and the cumin seeds and let it splatter for a couple of seconds. Take the pan off the fire and add the remaining chilli powder and stir for a minute. Pour this over the dal and serve hot.

SHALJUM DAL
[Turnips cooked in moong dal]

Serves: 4
Preparation time: 5 minutes
Cooking time: 20 minutes

Ingredients:

1 cup	moong dal [with its skin]
200 gms	turnips [cut in quarters]
1½ tsps	sugar
½ tsp	turmeric powder
1½ tsps	ginger juliennes
	salt to taste

For garnish:
[pour over the dal as garnish]

1½ tsp	clarified butter
¼ tsp	asafoetida
¼ tsp	cumin seeds
½ tsp	red chilli powder

Method:

Put the lentil, turnips, sugar, turmeric powder, fresh ginger juliennes and salt with 10 cups of water in a pressure cooker for 12 to 15 minutes [or till the turnips are tender but remain as whole quarters]. In a small pan heat the clarified butter. When it is hot add the asafoetida and the cumin seeds till it starts splattering. Take the pan off the fire and add the red chilli powder and stir for a second and pour over the dal as garnish.

KHATTI ARHAR DAL
[Sour arhar dal]

Serves: 4
Preparation time: 15 minutes
Cooking time: 25 minutes

Ingredients:

1½ cups	arhar dal
2	tomatoes – medium sized [finely chopped]
2 tsps	cooking oil
½ tsp	turmeric powder
	salt to taste
½ tsp	cumin seeds
½ tsp	asafoetida
¼ tsp	red chilli powder
1 tsp	ginger juliennes
2	green chillies [cut finely]
2 tbsp	lime juice extract
2 tbsp	fresh coriander [chopped finely]

Method:

Put the dal, turmeric powder, salt and 5 cups of water in a pressure cooker for 10 minutes till the grains have dissolved. Now whisk the lentil till it looks like a thick soup. In another pan heat the oil. When it is hot add the cumin seeds and the asafoetida and let it splatter for 2 minutes. Then add the chopped tomatoes, wait till the oil separates. Add the red chilli powder, ginger juliennes and chopped green chillies, stir for a minute or two and add to the cooked lentil. Finally, add the lime juice extract and chopped coriander and cook for another 5 minutes. Serve hot.

Dewan Pandit Motilal Atal of Jaipur (Jeypoor), my great grandfather's grandfather. Picture from the turn of the nineteenth century.

Arhar Dal

Serves: 4
Preparation time: 5 minutes
Cooking time: 15 minutes

Ingredients:

125 gms	arhar lentil
½ tsp	turmeric powder
¾ tsp	salt
1 tsp	fennel seeds [powdered]
1 ½ tsp	sugar

For garnish:

1 ½ tsp	clarified butter
¼ tsp	asafoetida
¼ tsp	cumin seeds

Method:

Put the lentil, turmeric powder, salt, fennel powder, sugar and 3 cups of water in a pressure cooker and cook for approximately 15 minutes, till the grains have dissolved. Whip the lentil with a whisk and add 2 ½ cups of water and cook for another 5 minutes on a medium flame without the lid, to get a thick soup consistency. In a small pan heat the clarified butter. When it is hot add the asafoetida and cumin seeds and let it splatter. Add this to the lentil just before serving.

SARVARI
[Chickpea pulao]

Serves: 2
Preparation time: 5 minutes
Cooking time: 20 minutes

Ingredients:

1 cup	basmati rice [washed]
¾ cup	chickpea [soaked overnight and boiled till tender]
3 tbsp	cooking oil
¾"	cinnamon stick
3	bay leaves
6	cloves
5	cardamoms [whole]
5½ cups	boiling water
	salt to taste

For garnish:

5	cardamoms [powdered]

Method:

Heat the oil in a pan. When it starts smoking add all the ingredients except the rice and chickpea and stir gently for a minute. Now add the rice and the chickpea along with 5 cups of boiling water and salt, and cook on a high flame for 5 minutes, then reduce to a low flame and cook for 10 to 12 minutes, till the water has dried [Do not stir the rice as the grains will break]. Garnish with cardamom powder.

BHASBHATTA
[Mixed vegetable pulao]

Serves: 2-3
Preparation time: 20 minutes
Cooking time: 40 minutes

Ingredients:

2 cups	basmati rice [wash & soak in water for 15 minutes]
1 cup	peas [shelled]
250 gms	cauliflower [cut in small flowerets and deep fried]
2	potatoes – medium sized [cut in halves and deep fried]
2 tbsp	cooking oil
½ tsp	cumin seeds
2	cardamoms
4 tbsp	ginger juliennes
½ tsp	asafoetida
2	bay leaves
1 tsp	mixed aromatic spice
2"	piece cinnamon stick
2	green chillies
1 tsp	red chilli powder
	salt to taste

Method:

Heat the oil in a pan and add the asafoetida and the cumin seeds. As the cumin seeds start browning add the rice and stir for a minute on a low flame. Gradually add the other ingredients, along with the spices and stir for a minute or two. Add 4½ cups of water and cover the pan. Cook over a low flame for 30 minutes, till the rice is tender.

KHAMEERI PURI

[Whole wheat pancakes cooked in milk and fennel seeds]

Serves: 4
Preparation time: 12 to 14 hours [should be done the night before]
Cooking time: 20 minutes

Ingredients:

1 ½ cups whole wheat flour
1 ½ cups refined flour
3 tbsp clarified butter
15 tbsp cooking oil [for frying the puris]
3 tbsp yeast
2 tbsp raw fennel seeds [powdered coarsely]
250 gms milk [warmed not hot]
salt to taste

Method:

Add the clarified butter to the whole wheat flour and the refined flour. Knead the mixture like a pastry gradually adding the warm milk, sugar, salt, yeast and the powdered fennel and make into a medium soft dough [If you need more liquid for the dough add warm water]. Knead the dough for at least 15 minutes till the yeast starts rising [at least 3 times the original dough]. Put the dough in the center of a pan and cover with a cloth [Leave overnight]. The next day. make balls from the dough and with a rolling pin make small pancakes [Approximately 10–12 cms in diameter]. You should get about 12–14 puris. Deep fry these pancakes in the cooking oil.

BARIA

[*Rice broth with black mushrooms*]

Serves: 4
Preparation time: 1 hour
Cooking time: 35 minutes

Ingredients:

¾ cup	basmati rice [washed]
1 tsp	asafoetida
½ tsp	cumin seeds
½ tsp	snow white lentil bari or Kashmiri flat bari ground to a powder
2 tbsp	mixed aromatic spices
15	almonds [soaked in water for 1 hour, peeled and halved]
2 tbsp	clarified butter
10	black mushrooms [washed, and soaked in water for 1 hour]
	salt to taste

For garnish:

2 tbsps	clarified butter
½ tsp	cumin seeds
½ tsp	asafoetida
¾ tsp	red chilli powder

Method:

Take 2 tablespoons of clarified butter in a pan and heat. Once hot add the asafoetida and the cumin seeds and let it splatter for a minute. Now add the snow white lentil bari, and stir for a minute. Add the rice and stir for a minute, gradually add the mixed aromatic spices with 5½ cups of water and let it cook for 20 minutes on a low flame. Once the rice is cooked mash it with a whisk and add 2 cups of water along with the mushrooms and almonds and salt to taste and leave on the fire for 10 minutes more till the consistency resembles a porridge. This is the baria.

For the garnish put the clarified butter in a pan and heat, add the asafoetida and cumin seeds. Once it splatters add the red chilli powder and immediately pour over the baria.

A portrait of Chitra Kaul, a paternal aunt at her wedding in 1949.

Chutneys, Raitas, Desserts

Aam ka gudamba
Navratan chutney
Kishmish raita
Meethi dahi
Meethe chawal
Phirni
Meethi guchi
Meethi khubani

AAM KA GUDAMBA
[Whole sweet mango chutney]

Preparation time: 25 minutes
Cooking time: 40 minutes

Ingredients:

2 ½ kg	raw green mangoes [peeled with the seed]
3 ½ kg	jaggery
2 tsp	asafoetida
2 tbsp	fennel seeds [slightly roasted]
2 tsp	red chilli powder
2 tbsp	wild black onion seeds
	salt to taste
1 litre	brown vinegar

Method:

Put the jaggery in a pan on the fire with 5 cups of water. When it starts melting take off the fire and strain through a muslim cloth. Take another pan and add all the other ingredients [except vinegar] along with the jaggery and cook on a slow fire for about 15 minutes. Gradually add the vinegar and let it cook till the consistency thickens. Remove from the fire, let it cool and pour into an air tight container. No refrigeration is required for the chutney and it can be kept for upto 6 months.

NAVRATAN CHUTNEY
[Sweet sour mango chutney]

Preparation time: 45 minutes
Cooking time: 35 minutes

Ingredients:

1 kg	raw green mangoes [grated, after discarding the skin and the seed]
4 tbsp	cumin seeds
1 tbsp	black pepper [coarsely powdered]
6 tbsp	ginger juliennes
¾ cup	raisins
20	green cardamoms [peeled & powdered coarsely]
1 kg	sugar
	red chilli powder to taste
	salt to taste

Method:

Put the raw green mangoes in a deep based pan on the fire and let it simmer for 10 minutes. Gradually add all the other ingredients and cook on a high flame for 5 minutes, stirring all the time. Put a lid over the pan and let it for 15 to 20 minutes, by which time the chutney will be cooked. It should be dark yellow in colour and the consistency should be like jam. Let it cool and pour into an air tight container. No refrigeration is required and the chutney can be kept for upto 6 months.

Kishmish Raita
[Raisin flavoured curd]

Serves: 3
Preparation time: 10 minutes

Ingredients:

3 cups	curd [whipped]
4 tbsp	raisins
½ tsp	sugar
	salt to taste
	pinch of red chilli powder
1 ½ tsp	cumin seeds [roasted and powdered finely]

Method:

Soak the raisins in warm water for 5 minutes. Drain out the raisins and add to the whipped curd. Now add the sugar and salt to the curd and stir well. Sprinkle red chilli powder and cumin powder on the curd as garnish. Serve chilled.

Meethi dahi
[Sweet curd]

Serves: 2
Preparation time: 5 minutes
Cooking time: 5 minutes

Ingredients:

3 cups	thick curd
¼ cup	sugar
6	green cardamoms [powdered]
1/8 tsp	saffron [crushed in 1 tsp of milk]
5 tsp	raisins [soaked in warm water for 2 minutes]

Method:

Beat the curds with sugar. Add the cardamom powder and saffron to the curd, and sprinkle the raisins. Serve chilled.

Meethe Chawal
[Sweet Rice]

Serves: 3
Preparation time: 15 minutes
Cooking time: 30 minutes

Ingredients:

1 cup	basmati rice [washed]
1 ¼ cup	sugar
2 tbsp	clarified butter
4	green cardamoms
6	cloves
1"	stick cinnamon

For garnish:

25	raisins
10	almonds [cut in slivers]

Method:

Boil the rice in a pan [not fully cooked – the grain should be slightly hard]. Drain the water and keep aside. Heat the clarified butter in another pan and add the cardamoms, cloves and cinnamon and cook for 5 minutes. Put the pan aside. Take a third pan and make a sugar syrup with 2 ½ cups of water [It should be of one string consistency]. Pour the sugar syrup and the clarified butter with spices over the rice and stir gently over a high flame for 10 minutes, then lower the flame and cook for another 5 minutes by which time the rice will have got soft and cooked. Garnish with raisins and almonds. Serve warm.

Phirni
[Rice Kheer]

Serves: 4
Preparation time: 10 minutes
Cooking time: 20 minutes

Ingredients:

8	cups milk
¾ cup	basmati rice [soaked in water over night]
½ cup	cold milk
1 cup	sugar
6	green cardamoms [peeled & powdered]
8	almonds [peeled & cut into slivers]

Method:

Soak the rice overnight, dry on a cloth and grind to a fine paste. Cook the milk on a slow fire for 5 minutes. Make a paste of the ground rice with a little cold milk and gradually add to the boiling milk, stirring all the time, so that lumps do not form. Cook this for 5 minutes. Now add the sugar and keep stirring. Cook for 5 minutes. Remove and cool, and mix half the powdered cardamoms and the slivers of almonds and sprinkle the rest on top.

Maj. Pyarelal Atal, my paternal great grandfather, who was killed in action in France during World War I, 30th November, 1914.

Meethi guchi

[*Sweetened black mushrooms*]

Serves: 4
Preparation time: 2 hours
Cooking time: 20 minutes

Ingredients:

100 gms	black mushrooms [soaked in water for 2 hours]
4 cups	sugar
10	pistachios [cut in juliennes]
	a generous pinch of saffron
10	green cardamoms [powdered]
20	almonds [soaked peeled & cut in slivers]

Method:

Take 3 ½ cups of water with sugar and boil till you get a one string consistency syrup. Now add the pistachios, saffron, cardamom powder to the syrup, along with the boiled mushrooms, and stir from time to time. Leave on the fire for 5 minutes and you should have your dessert ready. Serve cool, sprinkled with almond slivers.

Meethi khubani
[Sweet apricots]

Serves: 4
Preparation time: 15 minutes
Cooking time: 40 minutes

Ingredients:

1 kg	cottage cheese
1 ¾ cup	khoya [this is milk coagulated with a cheese like texture]
2 tsp.	soda bicarbonate
4 tbsps	cornflour
1 cup	castor sugar
1 ½ cups	almonds [soaked in water peeled & ground to a fine paste]
1 cup	dried apricots [boiled seeds discarded & retain the thick pulp]
10 tbsp	clarified butter [for deep frying]
	batasas [sugar dumplings]
	a pinch of salt
	a pinch of saffron
1 tsp.	kewara [essence for taste]

For the gravy:

8 cups sugar
20 green cardamoms [skin discarded & powdered]

For garnish:

1 tbsp almond slivers

Method:

Mix the khoya, cottage cheese, half the cardamom powder, soda bicarbonate, cornflour, castor sugar, almond paste, apricot pulp and a pinch of salt together and whisk for 10 minutes. Now take the batasas and cover it with the above mixture, making small balls [size a of lemon] and deep fry to a golden brown. Make a sugar syrup, with the sugar and equal quantity of water and add the remaing cardamom powder, saffron and kewara to it, once it is almost ready [the gravy shouldn't be too thin or thick]. Now add the golden fried batasas to the sugar syrup and stir gently for 5 minutes, so that the batasas don't break, and your dessert should be ready. Sprinkle with almond slivers.

Usha Atal, my paternal grandmother wearing traditional Kashmiri earrings [Ateheru]

Rs. 195/-
EWB 7648/13299
   HB
  ―――
  O₂+h